# The Machineries of Joy

# The Machineries of Joy

*Peter Finch*

Seren is the book imprint of
Poetry Wales Press Ltd.
57 Nolton Street, Bridgend, Wales, CF31 3AE
www.serenbooks.com
facebook.com/SerenBooks
twitter@SerenBooks

ISBN: 978-1-78172-565-8
ebook: 978-1-78172-566-5

A CIP record for this title is available from the British Library.

The publisher acknowledges the financial assistance of the Welsh Books Council.

Cover artwork: JimShoresArt
jimshoresart.com

Printed in Bembo by Bell & Bain, Glasgow.

# Contents

# Wales

Bigger than Texas,
fairer than Eire,
finer than Indochina,
redder than Belarus, faster than Andorra,
older than Mexico, slicker than Switz,
Frencher than France,
harder than the intifada,
more literate than Liechtenstein,
as moderate as Monaco, as hilly as Chile,
cleaner than Argentina, more beer than
Kashmir, more widgets than Egypt,
votes Labour like Jamaica,
not a failure like Australia, nor full
of plates like the States,
more cloudy than Saudi,
more drizly than Italy, as homely
as Estonia, more history than
Transnistria, as tribal as
the Bible, more weather than
the Netherlands, mightier than Haiti,
stronger than Uganda,
as lovely and holy as Mongolia,
once industrial now pastoral
like Norway, much craic like Iraq,
as sturdy as Cape Verde and about as British
as Mauritius.

Wales, hard to know.
Just when you think you do.
You don't.

# Things in the Western Sky

Buddha
Boundless
1024 millibars rising
Storm Cone
Skybolt
Cirrus
Saucer
West Minster migrant saint
Shed of air
The western skies are full of
Vapour crimson (why?) shards of ice
(delete shard) sheds of ice (substitute crisp)
Crisp shatter
Light full of translucent altocumulus
Shape of bone hoard
(add hymn)
Jehovah
Guide me
Pull me on

sky full of rain

sky full of light

# The Road West

Coming out of London on the elevated roadway
Amid the cameras from Orwell's future
west into sun

Radiohead on the player            I once thought
this was the revolution come back            but
turns out it wasn't

            The surface flattens
road full of local that'll drift off
as the land gets poorer and the chalk gives way
to green and brown

Beyond the cuttings are
trees, long abandoned hill forts cluttered with bushes,
scattered houses, pasture,   crop circles from
when the saucers were here   done overnight
by boys with skateboards and string listening
to the Roses    but now packed with
yellow rape and wavering corn.

In the vortex out there beyond Swindon
signboards to the anonymous  Works Exit
ill-favoured road leading to a
place whited-out on the OS maps      for weapon storage
a military fix      where post-nuclear
government control will sit      I wd have
felt annoyed once knowing that I was unsafe while
they were protected          cheered my brethren
there chained to the fences with their banners waving
but right now in the turbulent future who cares

The west

The downs. The long green-sided slide across
an England wider than I'd imagined with little
on it but frost.    A
million have done this so often, this crossing, it's a
walk in the park.  RS, up ahead land of his dust.

9

The trains sliding south of me that would have brought JT.
Bill Haley in 1957
Dylan once in a car before they built the bridge.

West

Over the water again the rocky
water sliding like a line of gunmetal suddenly
dug up      the bridge in its emerald shimmer
the sky      the seamless slip on to
where I'm going      a place much slower than it
once was    not everything always gets faster
and faster is not always better

The road still straight or the illusion of
that      with rain on it now and
the sun lost    arwyddion dwyieithog
they start       the angels of our west
                England finished
Wales instead.

# The Road West #2

And the road still west
clustered now with ancient names
they begin with bryn, allt, aber, llys,
    llyn, llwyn, & llan
    the landscape snuggling
    the hills looking down

Came here with Mac Low fresh up from America decades
back
    on some mash-up tour of fractured sound
me explaining the random to resistant audiences
    and him balancing books on his head

    the way is more vital
than the end – Alan Watts said

or something like

In the car we pick up a student
bound for home on her parents' Carmarthen farm
the veneer of slick fashion falling from her
as the trees thicken up.

I've got Diddley on some sort of 8-track Cliff
had fixed,    (it's his borrowed
car    no antifreeze)    and the temperature out there
is on its way down    pass the lights of the cities
    everywhere like frozen stars

We snap and click
        west    Diddley dum Diddley wha
west and
west again

where the roads finally end and the world
lies down  but god keeps on
    his towers pushing and his spires    the
smokestacks ran out miles back    the skies

are clear.     Mac Low hip flask gone slumbers in
the back          books in a bag

Those places where the docks were everything
and the land is scarred with steel mill and pit we've left them
and the bridges from which they hurled rocks at
the Polish truck drivers scabbing in coal in '84 and
then all those towns and cities full of the living filling
their heads with the stuff of nothing because
what else was there to do
we're beyond all that

west

where the land sits quiet and makes
        no comment

and the voices of the wild duck
are ever so faintly white

# Vote

*Democrat booth at the South Carolina State Fair,*
*beyond the Funnel Cake stand, next to the chickens.*

Well we ain't got her elected yet
but we're certainly gonna try.
You folk registered to vote, sure you are.
*Well yes, maybe,* I say, *but not here.*
You can tell other folk tho caint you you sure can.
Gonna give you this here bumper sticker.
Put that decal on front.
Republicans'll know we're wuppin em,
that's the plan.

But in the event Judy Gilstrap goes down.
God fearing Eric Bikas, owner of popular
local tourist destination Aunt Sue's Country
Corner on Highwy 11 in Pickens he wins.
Didn't see him at the State Fair wasn't there
got his votes by other means.

Given a testament at the Gideon's stall next door.
Man in a white shirt like a Mormon said the Church of
England's fucked. Didn't use that word, quite,
I paraphrase. *You a Republican,* I ask?
Sure and even if I wasn't I would be. This
is the south and the Land of the Free.

Not one dark face in the entire fair and only
a single sign in Spanish. *Tacos El Paraiso $2*
White folk in shirts and tattoos and cowboy hats.
As far as the eye can see.

# On the Road Again

*the 40 then the 61 USA 2010*

On The Road Again
In Memphis buying shoeshine kits at Schwab's
Corncob pipes    Thermal drawers
Bongo drums    Pillbox hats
Crystal balls
Back scratchers    Electric flashers
Carnival beads    Inflatable weeds
Mojo lotions    Voodoo potions
Dinosaurs    Barbecue sauces
Flap-end hunter's hats    Mecca mats
Praying hands    Desert sands
Christian ties    All-seeing eyes
Negro treats    Boiled sweets
3-D glasses    Cowboy hats
Ras-clad gloves    Graceland knockers
Packets of gum    Things you strum
Leg shavers    Jumbo erasers
Rocking robin    Stop your sobbin
Hair extensions
Wall Street braces    Rainbow chasers
Bib and tuckers    Hammers, nails
Inflatable whales
Nobama stickers    Frogs leg clickers
Peaches in tins    Books of hymns
Mangle handles    Beatnik sandals
Lonely rooms    Cheese moons    Iron lockers
Plugs    Chains    Negro statues
Oil    Toil    Laughing tomatoes
Big O glasses    Cut-out dolls
Pirate patches
Mobile Blues    Platform Shoes
Pointed bras    Dust
Dust    lots of dust
On the road again
On the road
again

On the Road Again
past Churches
The Infinite God
The Alice Bell
The Atkins Believers
The Basswood Baptists
The Beaver Creek
Calvary United
Church of Christ
Church of God
Clinch River
Tallahatchie Fervour
Church of Grace and Glory
Church of Back-Sliders
The wrecked and forlorn
The Waving Arms
The sweat on the brow
Hot Damn Big Rock
Boulder City Corn Cob
Missionary Followers of Jesus
Man with the Flowing Beard
Beard beard
They shall all have beards
Church of the Serpent
The Great Redeemer
Ebenezer on Kingston Pike
God in the Pines
Church of the Pouring River
Hold me brother
Let me sing
On the road again
On the road
again

On The Road Again
hearing
Muddy    Howlin
Crippled    Blind Boy
Hard-Armed    Pegleg

Stovepipe    Sonny
Big Time  Wild Child
Bumble Bee
T-Model    H Bomb
Quickslide    Homesick
Enormous Sundown
Lucky    Watermelon
Whistlin Lil Son Smokey
Nail-bomb
Jones    Williams    Thomas    Washington
Johnson    Taylor    Aberdare    Edwards
Wales    –    None ofem ever heard othat country  nosir
All been to the Abertillery  Blues Fest
Said they had a great time
On the road again
On the road
again


On the Road Again
Bethesda Alaska
Canton Oklahoma
Everywhere
Or maybe nowhere

On the road
Again

# Clarksdale

*I went down to the crossroad,*
*fell down on my knees.*
*I went down to the crossroad,*
*fell down on my knees.*
*Asked the Lord above, "Have mercy now,*
*Save poor Bob, if you please."*

I got there
pulled in next to the gas station where the homeboys
snap their fingers, stopped
in the forecourt of a wrecked frigerator store,
fogged after five-hundred miles down 61
expecting a monument found a
cut-out guitar on a road-island pole.
No Welcome to Clarksdale cotton town.
No mention of Robert Leroy Johnson selling his
young man's soul in exchange
for  forty-one incandescent sides.
At the record store they tell me that the only blues
on live tonight is white stuff,  okay you know,
been like that for a while.
John Lee Hooker Lane empty, Muddy's shack moved on.
They've got his guitar in a museum,
next to Charlie Musslewhite's shoes.
The blues ain't nothin' but, big legged momma,
down in this delicious delta.
Only now they're dead-end history.
Ghost riders.
On the car stereo their
memory rattles and hums.

# Ty Draw

The hill is sharper, but the house is smaller.
Its front renovated, sand blasted, repainted
although its door, the one where most
memory resides, stays lawnmower green. I must
have crossed this threshold a thousand times.

On up  a neighbour in socks is being told
the bad news about his slates from a roofer
poking in the eaves from the scaffold. Where
the cutting once was is now a hedge and a row
of crisp semis shimmering their double glazing
at the brand-new world. Are there traces I
might have left from a whole childhood
spent living here? Initials carved into a post,
a damaged window sill, some ghostly
motes floating still in the Roath Park air?

Nothing.

Round the back where the past might
still congeal among the rust and residue
they've renewed almost everything.
I once painted my name on
the lane tarmac in front door green
but the rains have long washed it. In a life
how much do you have to do to outlive it?
They kept chickens next door and I
loved them but today no sound
remains.

A door opens and a face asks me
what I'm doing here where housebreakers
would walk. I say chasing the
past. I used to live here. Do you remember me?
He shakes his head.

But at the top of the hill there's
smoke from the train, still rising,
as it trucks its coal to the dockland sea.
I can see it, smell it, hear its gouts of grey
and black. Smuts. Steam. On and back.

I've written it now.
And you've read it. So, something remains.

# The Psychic Triangle

*Where the lines of Cardiff's waters cross and the leys*
*and roads intermingle—the past and present of the city. This is it.*

the river is a distant slumber
the feeder is a hollow tube
the gorsedd is a grafted ganglion
the path is a devious shoe
the river is a drizzled timemixer
the city is a hovering hoop
the city is a mabinogi murmuring
the city is a leaden soup
the city is a brewage grumble
the city is a biscuit stumble
the judge is a spinning rover
the martyrs are airborne refrigerators
the city is a visible lover
the canal is a lossy compression
the river is a blinding sparrow
the canal is a lost originator
the river is a bardic marrow
the feeder is a diamond geezer
the fountain is a  tourniquet trembling
the lost are blinding regulators
the ley is an engineered teaser
the road is a religious resistor
the martyrs are trembling dockworkers
the water is a photocopied freezer
the feeder is a fish feeler
the feeder is an arterial renovator
the feeder is an elevated intelligentsia
the feeder is a geisha ghost
the river is a bowdlerised teacher
the feeder is a fixed failure
the feeder is a fascinating frightener
the feeder is a forecasted financier
the feeder is a financial filibuster
the feeder is a phishing finisher
the feeder is a filo footballer
the feeder is a Philadelphian foot-fixer

the feeder is a time-mixed corrupter
the feeder is a boatless elongation
the feeder is a saline resistor
the city is a gorgeous Goodway
the city is a rolls Rickenbacker
the city is an echoing encrustation
the city is a mind melder
the city is a molten conception
the city is an historical footballer
the city is a mended mastication
the city is a fixed  mirror

a haircut, a decompressed chest, a shining brick,
a steelworks, a marquis, a fixer,
a brick grip, a brick slide, a brick slip,
the city is a  such a slick creation

# Death Junction

*Roath Brewery (clsd 2018) had this on the
label of its dark beer*

a beer for where Roath rubs against Cathays
where cut throats and the gibbet and the gallows pit
were once the only future

★

where Richmond meets Mackintosh
where the crwys uncrossed
where Albany hits Plwca
where the dead walked
where the lost were defiled and the criminal met their ends
drink to their memory. they'd  love that.

# The City Region

Tidefields Road, Tydfil Place, Ty Draw Road, Carisbrooke Way, Grand
Avenue, Boulevard de Nantes, Stuttgart Strasse, Fort Street, Mallards
Reach, Brook View, The Ashes, The Oaks, The Willows, The Birches,
The Elms, The Conifers, The Alders, The Willows, the Trees of Heaven,
The Bushes from Hell, The Pines, Hill Street, Hot Street, Ho Street,
Queen Street, King Street, Princes Street, Presidents Way, Potenti-
ate Plaza, Steam Street, Zinc Street, Tin Street, Diamond Street,
Silver Street, Emerald Street, Iron Street, Lead Street, Pearl Street,
Uranium Plaza, Whinberry Way, Mount Stuart Square, MacDonald
Crescent, Heol Llangynidr, Heol Llangattock, Heol Llanbedr, Heol
Llanilltud, Molten Road, Milton Street, Monster Strasse, Wordsworth
Avenue, Coleridge Plaza, Heol Trelai, Minhinnick Strasse, Curtis Way,
Cowbridge Road, Roughage Lane, Seawall Close, Market Road, Tidal
Sidings, Freshmoor Street, Froth Street, Meteor Street, Planet Street,
Comet Street, Eclipse Street, Van Allen Boulevard, Keuiper Way, Oort
Avenue, Karmen Place, Humboldt Street, Hottentot Road, Harris
Bypass, Jenkins Way, Williams Street, Thomas Street, Jones Street, Price
Street, Preston Street, Dunleavy Street, Goodway Plaza, Willows Square,
Bute Way, Bute Street, Bute Road, Bute Strasse, Bute Place, Bute
Walk, Bute Dance, Bessemer Road, Vulcan Square, Dowlais Avenue,
Merthyr Road, May Street, Moira Street, Minny Street, Letty Street,
Gladys Street, Fanny Street, The Plaza, The Plaza, The Plaza. The Plaza.

# Hendrix Island

Near the lake island in what was once
a malarial swamp
the fallen tree is fenced
its pollarded bulk like a broken car.

Last summer in a storm of psychogeography
I brought the bike tour here
told them about Hendrix waking on that islet
no idea how he arrived
or where he was.
there's a plaque now    fantasy memorialised    island edge
they all nod        I read a lyric
the past a palimpsest fictioned
into fashionable fact

I read the event reported later
internet somewhere
as if it happened
real now (slight return)
yes yes.

# City

As a city it often thinks about itself
out there among the galloping winds.
Has it got its towers straight?
Its malls glow  like venial sins.
It knows what it is.  It has put its name
up in a shouting bilingual rash
all over its face.

It is a place of beguiling sparkle and
drunken slash.  It runs in my veins.

As a city it wonders how it ever changed
with its docks a pasteurised echo and
its workers without a lump of hard skin
on any of their hands.
Its history hangs about it like rags.

Here's a list of its rivers: the Taff, the Ely, the
Rumney, the Roath, the Tan, the Canna, the Wedal,
Nant Glandulas, Nant Ty Draw. They all rush
to the sea where there are still tides and salt.
There the ships that made this place once sailed
but now do not.  But on its bed of silt
behind its barrage walls the city still floats.

# Ways To Get To God

ablutions, scarifications, scarmongerings, prostrations, recitations, conversations, righteous interjections, confessions, petitions, meditations, devotions, contemplations, infusions, elevations, visitations from archangels, enervations, assassinations.

# Train

click clack click clack
click clack click clack

come back baby
come back

on this train  were once

click clack

men in khaki going to war
the Royal Mail swiftly sorting
thick suits and wide news papers
men with pipes smoking
kids with fever, lovers courting
hoards with cases,  excited faces
smog and frosts that
split the soil and froze the rivers
lampless roads and unlit paths,
the train a stream of shining glory,
the roll and rattle, the whistle scream,
the chattering points the sway and thwack
click clack click clack click clack
no health and safety,
no Radiohead, no Nelly Furtado,
no Ice T, no Dizzee Rascal,
no Lily Allen, no Cate Le Bon,
no Super Furries,
no lager can shambles, no maps
no speaker reminder to remember
to get off get on stand back start back
click clack click clack click clack.

Trains to everywhere  −  Peterstone
Blaenrhondda, Pulford, Crawley,
Redmire,  Sigglesthorne, Slinfold,
Shepherdswell, Sexhow, Seven Sisters,
Swadon, Scalby, Scorton,
Nannerch, Nantclwyd, New Cut Lane, Littlestone,

Llanfalteg, Llanfyrnach, Llandulas, Llangelynin, Llong,
Merkland, Boxford, Speke, Speen, Spellow
Wall, Wark, Wrexham Central,
Wittyon-le-Wear, Wooler, Withyham,
Gosport, Yeldham,   Hope, & Pen-y-Ffordd
to anywhere but no longer.

In the coaches they are phoning home.

You know what they've saying.

Blue Train, Freight Train,
Love Train, Peace Train, Mystery Train,
The Train I Ride, The A Train,
This Train, That Train, Train Train,
Trick Train, Track Train, Main Train,

click clack click clack

Night Train,  Right Train, Rich Train,
Rock Train, Deep Train, Dark Train,
Dope Train, Real Train, Trane Train,
Wet Train, Wobble Train, Slow Train,
Snow Train, Smack Train, Packed Train,
This Train, Pissed Train, Welsh Train.


click clack click clack     click

# The Pursuit of Happiness

This is something we should know by now is futile. Time wasted in the
lanes looking for the cats. As dusk came I used a mini Maglite
to peer under bushes and into those slots between houses where bins
cluster and abandonment mixes with loss. I called names but
got no response. I wanted the happiness of discovery
to flood my neural channels enough to lift me from my shoes
but I remained  rooted to the ground. Life is short and full of suffering.
The Buddha said conquer yourself and the suffering will end. I
told the cats this once and they purred at the revelation.
Struggle on then cease. I turn the Maglite off.
I compose the poster I will tomorrow deliver
to all local houses, pin on trees and string from lampposts. Put
through doors. It will have a photograph and a heartfelt plea.
Already I sense my place on the eight-fold path.  In the dark
among the buddleia there is a rustle
and there they are, whiskers, noses, tails,
coming back.

# The Tree

Spent the morning looking up
what this new drug I'm taking might be doing
none of the information good.

Outside where my father would have admired
the way I've painted the wall, white to push
light across the grass, stands the tree.    Smaller
than his Eiffel Leylandii which took
paid men to trim but still high enough to
need ladders and guts.

We stood out here once.  Or somewhere
similar.  Him like smoke, me like frost.  He told me
his hands no longer worked but that
such things now didn't matter.  We stayed
for a while until the chill sent us back.

You don't need that tree.  He said that.
It looks at me now in its fullness, its
defiant vertical green, its bulbous
mutinous growth.  And driven
by whatever it is that's in
my failing veins I decide to cut.
I haul out the ladder and the shears and
get up there nearer the sun to whirl
at it, foliage like rain, leaves and dust.

When I'm done and in the prednisolone
users chat room where a woman has
just told us that she's put on eighteen
pounds and another that she gets
panic attacks even bringing in the milk
I write that  I've turned the branched fan
vaulting of a blue green evergreen  into a
containable ball and that my father  is out there
where the great gardeners go
waving his secateurs and laughing.

# The Voyage of Dementia

The voyage of discovery
The victim of disaster
The volume of dissonance
The vileness of dementia

The discovery of shelter
The death of simplicity
The dissonance of democracy
The disaster of decisions

The viciousness of critics
The volume of criticism
The voyage of creation
The vision of cremation

The dimness of vicissitude
The demonstration of volume
The debility of ventilation
The death of vision

The fracture of the future
The firmness of failure
The flux of fullness
The filibuster of death

The criticism of creation
The commuting of conquest
The courage of consolation
The cessation of commutation

The diagram of diplomacy
The digitisation of drumming
The dimness of dignity
The disregard of depth

The directness of the dharma
The diagnosis of devaluation
The death of desperation
The dementia of denouement

The denouement of dementia.

# Stigmata

Outside the hospital the patients
are showing each other their
wounds. They take off their gowns
which are thin and have lettering
on the breast and drape them
over the signs which warn against
smoke. Do not light up.
Tobacco is forever banned.
All around the cherry
trees are full of small chirping birds.
One patient has a mark like a
stigmata on his arm. Another a
drain in his side which ends in a
great sagging  bag. Sunken-faced
they breathe as if the world of joy
was about to end. The air
is a miasma of grey. Nobody objects.
Even the doctors when they pass by
in their scrubs stay silent.
These physicians are thinking
only of painless cure. The patients
of phantasmal angels and
the slow path to death.

# Bladder

In the clinic the bladder is king
a bright thing, full of bliss.

I watch the doors along the corridor open to
usher out the desperate and the damned
who've just been told; once calm and
unwitting now shaking with despair.

Age here is ubiquitous except me
a decade back when I first arrived but now me also
fragile and stumbling, waiting in line.

The doctors have lives outside all this
where they grow beans like green razors
and play squash in titanic volleys
sweat and breath filling them with joy.

But today they have their caring
voices in their mouths telling
us slowly where the pathology
leads. X-rays on their screens
like Bacon paintings
a grapefruit in cross section
filled with demon papillary,
dark markers where
earlier manifestations have been
taken away.

We will have to see how
it progresses they tell me
like builders saying we've fixed
it, we think,
see how it goes, wait till it rains.
All aspects of bladder work
undertaken no job too big
no job too small.

Fill it with bitumen. Blowlamp it.

Outside as ever it rains.

# Bone

These are the things

all white bone
chalk white bone
flake white bone
cream white bone
sea white bone
pale white bone
bone white bone
lax white bone
wash white bone
powder white bone
lime white bone
soft white bone
gloss white bone
bride white bone
hat white bone
paper white bone
quartz white bone
light white bone
mist white bone
honk white bone
jet white bone
hard white bone
old white bone
cloud white bone
bleach white bone
thin white bone
weak white bone
woven white bone
dust white bone
bone the colour
of light then bone
the colour of bone

# Boots

The sound of the man next door getting
out of bed with his boots already on
is really my Uncle Billy who was
killed by a shunted brake van and who I
never knew. He came home from the
yards last night with a belly full of
beer. The chattering radio seeping up through the
chimney cavity is actually my grandmother,
the one who fell off a bus and cracked her head
dead, sweeping the house clean of
anything new that might have
got in on the bottom of someone's
shoe. The electricity leaking
from the sockets and running over
the floor like invisible lino is all still
there. She feared it. So too the phone in the
hall which she never used. She grappled with the
twentieth century by denial. The
Titanic still sails. They are not on the moon.
Billy isn't dead at all. He goes out and
up the road in those boots just like
the man next door. If she could
my grandmother would run after
him with his packed lunch and a
tartan flask of tea. But she can't
because she's dead as well.

# The Waiting List

This is true. Cn't do.
ncrsngly oldr slowr
cnt run too cnt run to.
climb strs breath breathe don't do. wnt too.
try huff enormous heft breath also too
wef wheez  whes wheeze won't do.
cant do. cant do. nt like it used to.  true.
I'd lke n appntmnt  6 mnths wait. bg htch.
box nhs app do. six pg tck which box x do.
have you sffrd any of these?  tck all.
I tck all all. are all ths you?   they are
they are  they are   true
hd staight to th head of th head of th head of
th head of th head of th head of th
waitng waitng
waitng dr will see you now
queue.

# He's Sixty Foot Tall

In the school yard they are
discussing god over a game
of marbles. He's a big man
sixty foot tall I've seen him
in the night carrying off strayed
people says a lad with
orange frizz. No he's
not says another with a thin face
pale like he had a weak heart,
you can't see him he's just there,
floating. But it's the fat
kid with the hands like porkers
who's got it, there's no god stupid,
he cries, smashing the small
glass alleys asunder with his
his great silver bomber ball.

# I Have No Idea What The Answer Is

My father said everything would always get
better  but it did not.
His brother  had a fortune in
chickens lined-up for the back gardens
where we lived.  Streets
which hadn't seen husbandry for
years.  But the feathers failed.  We
tried to put  a turbine on
the roof to kick-start my son's
business.  The winds were strong
but the grants were sand.    I
have no idea what the answer is.
A visitor's guide advises that brown
coins are worthless  so lose them.
Hopeless.  Yet somehow
out there in the grey world
things are still going on.

# Get A Job

They'd lined up these jobs on the blackboard:

Engineer
Furnaceman
Builder
Clerk

In white chalk. That last one'll suit you, son,
it's indoors. You go
down there to the City Hall and ask.
They want bright ones like you.
No one will let molten steel run on your
shoes or collapse the mine roof on your head.
You can keep your hands pink. The
sky outside was riddled with smut. I went
and I asked and I was in. Columns of
figures, ink. The boss told
me keep your jacket on, don't sing.
Filled in a form in yellow light. Made
a list of those who had come to
licence their dogs and hand over rates.
Collected the money. Added it up.

Things I did:

Learned to talk.
Discovered the size of the City. Not big.
Clock.
Ink pad, lever arch, filing tag.
Williams, Davies, Jones, Davis,
Abdullah, Smith.

That list sounded good.

Didn't know it,
but I'd started out.

# Wild Wales

### Dining
For salmon Berwyn eaten the river Ireland full a leg tasted
never the turn let fection only exception inferior here for at
we Llangollen very ale cottage in the neighbourhood of mutton

### Serpents
On the to I on the making returned a which of which short
asked could If lines are I good two old archdeacon and poetry
verbing I am mightily of the voice small men mostly

### Genius
The family Llangollen birthplace works Goronwy 1722 parents
they ever he celebrated became natural benefit at where Col-
lege ing guished gave gauge after in Wales the embarrassments
were always the brightest ornaments

### Poverty
In life of ludes like lude of English Poetry courses change more
century called styled were posed monk verses visions visions
visions rank long eateries and France Incarnation moralities spo-
ken Doctor holds some interludes allegory display in modern
manners yes no have to agree no single shoe rope belt sack
blouson trousers

### Rivers
and from precipice cataract upper pass through waters romantic
hollow bourhood with wood penetrate piece on dingle Rheidol
one the about the to children and nearly stroyed at however
nature but last (always last) and position into is frightfully terri-
bly and soak showers neverending

### Heaven
they the which and thing were from for hindity morning well
as farewell giving in won't hold vile old gentleman I was very
becoming little village of ing who Capel rather English man I
was I I myself prayed paradise paradise was steep more steep
than ever and then a benighted paradise translation

# The Machineries of Joy

Bach and his student assistant have set up
their machineries of joy at the end of
the pet food aisle at Sainsbury's.   They
offer industrial quantities of
symphony and sonata ready packaged
to all-comers but there are few today.
A woman with a home-knit cardigan
and NHS-issue stick admonishes J. S.
for being way too productive.  Her husband's
many concerti, she complains,
don't sell as they once did. This is,
she says, because Bach's cost less.  Outside in
the sky a great wheel of seagulls
circle.  The drinkers on the benches
slumber.  At home a bald bent man sits
in his room writing on sheaves of stave
paper.  This is his obsession.
He knows it is all ultimately pointless
because the kids don't listen anymore,
if they ever did,
but he doesn't care.

# First Hearing Bob Dylan Baby Let Me Follow You Down from the First Album so many Years Ago they are almost Gone

That was around here, somewhere,
and the song stays,
wave on wave, in the billowing air.
It's cogent & creased & crawling,
faint[1] in the space between atoms,
repeating itself further and further.
It's out there now beyond Venus
e string rattling the universe's dust.

I read that the far far future when this world's gone
would be a pea soup of broken particle undulating
stretched from here to god and back
in one blue bend.  Lepton, fermion, boson,
plekton, plasmon, hadron,  sigma bottom, charmed prime,
blind boy grunt's exciton, bob zimmerman's quark.

I put my ear to the wind.
The song's still there I can hear it
strange and full of charm.

[1] *Israel Zangwill writing in the Pall Mall Magazine in the 1890s suggested that nothing was ever lost. "Time is perpetually travelling through space, repeating itself in vibrations farther and farther from the original point of incidence…. a succession of sounds that, having once been, can never pass away."*

# Crow

*(for Doped in Stunned Mirages: A Poetic Celebration
of Don Van Vliet, Liverpool, 2017.)*

is the desert deserted
is the Mojave green
is the radar realistic
is the rollo rolled
is the host the most
is the holy    oly    oh
is black a colour
is money a failure
is the sky true    true oh
is blue a bottle fly
is it as big as a cowboy eye
is eternity a skeleton breath
is the sun free
is cotton pop
is the poop a hatch
is the shepherd a trumpet
is suncream icecream pope cream
is a pipe a peep
is silence smoke
is the show stoppable
is the crow cawing oh oh hello
is the day rope
is it weeping
is it a reaper
is the main offence the main event
is the past really tense
is fission articulate
is a noggin elastic matriculate
is the sun unstable unusable
is the carpenter carpenterising my bones
is time tight and able
is the stream a bable babel
is the moon strong
is the mask pure
is the piano certain
is carbon paper

is red that's it
is hope getting old
is the poem sell selling sold
is the skeleton full of intent
is most of the host the most holyo
is the head  math math plastic
is god in vain to slaughter
is the dark a mercy daughter
is the brother singing on truth mountain
is the cranium cracked
is the brainium  mastic
is the noggin a classic
is the class an antic
is this a keeper
is the vent a fountain
is now when it's steeper
is it peaceful out there in antique land
is the  desert  ocean dried
is this poem personifying
is it wide
is it perambulating by day
is it perambulating by night
is this poem right
is this poem hot
is this pome a keeper
is this pome a failure
is this pome a feature
is this pome a crow
is it missing impossible can't be arsed to spend the money
is the pome imperfect past tense verbal  shopping bags
is the pome just a moan
is the moon a stone
is the sky dark in daytime
is ice cream for crow   oh
is the host an idea
is destruction retaliation
is blood forgotten
is the head a hat
is music the lack of silence oh silencio
is the crow christ turning
is the crow a baptist burning

is it south of something
is it learning
is it art why ask
is chess a cerebal tactic
is the past the main fanatic
is the mp three of them
is brine that vile
is the cranium malicious
is the brain mathematical
is it really chuzz chuzz
is lipwork possage pilfer
is magicman plinleered
it is youngleigh light
is jomp a lerrkmmmmp
is a distraktengivor a bengingpop
is a toomwow a yeaning bone
is a menmann gardes lomp
is creakslis fanapzwash oh
is a salerang unda beatlum greal growl wow toasio
is heartbustingflip
is nonstap vliet vliet
is fishfled flags
is wishta ta rag
is crowful longgonongham
is glad flijouy
is flomgsd flaggs
is fat loompnoph creamo fat
is hat gads westlig for the main even  t
is hsfdomdom sloss tross ss
is news os suu ususus s
is gadsas s
is flodsd ss ssgss hsf vr
is testraljss tsssghdes ss desssss sssssjs sss
is sflossfgssssjss sssss ssss sshgs
is ssssjs sss sssskss ssssksss
is sssss sssss ssssslss sss ss
is sss sssss ssssss sss sssss s ss sssk
is ssss ssssss sss ss sssss sss ss s
is s ssss sssssks ssss sssssss s ssssss
is s ssssssssss sssssssssss ssss ssss
is s ssss sssss sssss s ss ssssks sssss

45

is ss sssss ss ssssssssssssss sssssss s sssss
is sss sssssss sss ssss
is ssssssssssssss sssssss sssss ssssssss
is sss ssssssss sss ssss
is ssssssssss ssssssss ssss ssssssssss
is ssssssssssss ss sss ssssssssssssssssssssssk
is ssssssssssssssssssssssssssssssssss sssssss
is sss sssssssssssssssssssssssssssssss ssss
is ss ssssssssssssssssssssss sssssssssssss ss
is sssssssssssssssssss sssssssssssssss
is ss ssss ssss
is sssssssssssssssss sssssssss
is s ssssssssssssssssssssssssssssssssssss
is ss ssssssssssssssssskssssssssssssssssss s
is sssssssssssssssskssssssssssssss
is ssssssssssssssssssssssssssssssssssss
is sssssssssssssssssssss
is sssssssssssss
is sssssssssssssssss sssss
is ss sssssssssss sssssssssssssks
is ssssssssssssssssssssssss
is sssssssssssss
is sssss
is ssssss
is ssssss
is sssssssssssssss
is sssssssssssssssssssss
is sssssssssss
is sssssssssssssssssss
isssssssssssss
sssssssssssssssssssssssssss
ssssssssssssssss
sssssssssss
sssssssssss
sssssssssss
ss
s

s

s

ss

sss

ss

s

Peter Fin sh sssssss s o

# White

Rather  than *The White Album*
it was *The Great White Wonder.*
In '69 I couldn't understand why the
world didn't just go on making more
money instead of trying to end itself in fire

rolled marbles under the hooves of
horses    Pentagon surrounded with flowers
kept heading on and higher
om mani padme
roundhouse hum

um  then  revlt nm um revoil nub  rr rev  ine
n br in br mthr nnn ure sun son soon sun
n n bk bk bk bk back t bck in t t
back in the in t tr tr trrr you eee trrr ss
ess ess ess ess bungalow bungalow – number 9 – mk onk ess ss
blu rac n hon hon hon e mmm rus wa wall oo hare dum

started to disband Jesus echo snt back har hare
leaving minimal found bed in white suit infatuati
roof plas tur krrr kclap clap crm crum
wish piece  cut piece  voice piece  arse film
hide until everybody dies

Duchamp as rock star

after that all done

*The White Album released Nov 1968*
*The Great White Wonder released July 1969*

# The Insufficiency
# Of Christian Teaching
# On the Subject Of
# Common Emotional Problems

Exiited Peperit Filivms

Vum Primo Genitum

et reclinavit vot          oot at tossed

General    Gentian    Chrysanthemum

mmmmmmmmmmum        arr    um

hic    ic    ee          oooooom
        ic  ee  eee
        incet  arturus
    Arthur rather Arthur
        Artur Artur
    Artur odenm king
        Senatus
        seething
seething  seething  seething
seething  seething  seething
seething  seething  seething
        seething
        sing

rrrrrrrrr

# R

diddle  ip

tip ip  trip tip
ip  ip  ip  ip
eeeeeeeee  ip  ip

Christian bogus
Celtician transition
renovate  rendition
elevate patrician
pwy yw duw oooooo
hollol
ollol  ollol

no answer yet

# Stein

*3 Feb, 1874 – 27 July, 1946*

You are here in the ground of
Père Lachaise beneath a stone
big enough to hold you down. The space
around you is full of names you'd know,
Max Ernst, Paul Eluard, Modigliani, de Nerval,
Perec, Proust, Pissarro, Wilde, Appolinaire, Alice B.
This is no humble place, it's a city.
To get around you need a map.

Given what you did I expected uproar like Morrison gets.
Sad-eyed ladies of the lowlands, young men
with revolution inside their heads. But there's nothing.
It's as if you'd not changed the twentieth at all
challenged its serial monogamy made it
ripple with how the brain turns.
There's no bramble nor trees near you,
no ivy growing across your name.
Just a rose someone has left,
shrivelled now, and a stone in the
shape of a heart dropped above
where yours might be.

Old and young and gone and gone
Gone forever old old old I was I was
it's forever ever and ever just like this.

# Second Aeon Magazine in Numbers

*second aeon poetry journal edited by Peter Finch 1966–1974.*

twenty twenty
nineteen sixty-five
nineteen eighty-four
nineteen forty-seven
five hundred
fourteen and ten
nineteen fifties
two thousand and one
two thousand and ten
two and six
eight to the bar (beat me)
twelve stone two pounds
half a mile
fifty percent of a hectare
third of a pint
a galleon a gallon a gaggle a grasp a grip
three point one four one five one nine
six nineteen sixty sixty sixty sixty six

ten guineas print bill
a four seventy  Manor Way
Church Road turn left
Station Road, Llandaf North
The Pineapple.  Led to second aeon brite yellow
64-mil hard sized sixteen foolscap pages
two staples (rust) William Wantling
Glyn Jones Wm Burroughs Kingsley Amis (said no)
Redgrove many American stars and European
Concrete-ists Welsh wizards English poetasters.
Criticised for spelling the name dom sylvester houedard
three different ways in the same issue.
nineteen seventy-four sold three thousand copies
a thousand more in a box   issue nineteen
to twenty-one big boy cover by Tony Rickaby
Wales replete (Pwy yw'r twat hwn? Lol)
none left now took nearly forty years
eye ess ess enn zerozero threeseven dash zerotwentyfive

copy in the loft foxed illegible

my last one.

# Institutions of Wales #1

assembly assembly assembly assembly assembly
assembly assembly assembly assembly assembly
assembly assembly assembly assembly assembly
assembly assembly assembly assembly assembly
assembly assembly assembly assembly assembly
assembly assembly assembly assembly assembly
assembly assembly assembly assembly assembly
assembly assembly assembly assembly assembly
assembly assembly assembly assembly assembly
assembly assembly assembly assembly assembly
assembly assembly assembly assembly assembly
assembly assembly assembly assembly assembly
assembly assembly assembly assembly assembly
assembly assembly assembly assembly assembly
assembly assembly assembly assembly assembly
assembly assembly assembly assembly assembly
assembly assembly assembly assembly assembly
assembly assembly assembly assembly assembly
arsembly assembly assembly assembly assembly
assembly assembly assembly assembly assembly
assembly assembly assembly assembly assembly
assembly assembly assembly assembly assembly
assembly assembly assembly assembly assembly
assembly assembly assembly assembly assembly

# John Ashbery Visits Lidl

Everyone loved what they saw.
The rough displays, the mitre makers
The marigolds and the clothes
The persimmon velvet curtains
The garlic tea cloths
The passionate biscuits
The Slavonic chocolate
The wines from Cricklewood and Westphalia

The whole family are keenly interested
They arrive in droves.

The first year was like icing
The man with the red hat
The girls protected by gold wire
The music that never ceased.
Now they swear by tennis balls
the unknowable crispbreads, the meats in vacuum packs.

Sometimes they come because their cars do
Sometimes they are profligate
Sometimes they are radiant
Sometimes they shop because there is little else to do
Mostly though it's pedantic Cindy without brio or élan.

The family they just want to save money
They always do
They have this furious passion.

They buy onions
They buy the weirdly branded tins,
the fold-up beds, the spread-on chocolate,
the fun size spanners.

Clearly the song will have to wait
amongst all this great saving
How brave they are
buying Marigolds when at home they have dozens.

In the queue there he is but no one recognises him
why would they, the joker,
self-portrait in his trolley,
his New York face peering out of that so realistic convex mirror.

# Ready Availability

*Charles Dickens Bicentenary 2012*

The Bachelor the Bachelor the Barnacles the Bachelor the Badger
Dedlock (Dartle)(Drummle)(Duff) Cripples (Crimple)(Crupp)
Cupcake (Caught) Creakle (Gradgrind)(Grimwig)(Gulpidge)(Great)
Rokesmith (Rudge)(Rudge)(Rudge)(Rudge)(Real)(Rug)
Sloppy (Slowboy)(Slightboy)(Slammer) Situation (Speculative)(Slight)
the Warden the Warden (Wardle)(Wardle)(Waterbrook)
Wopsle (clerk)(friend)(actor)(thesb.)(fame)(luck)
Plornish (plasterer)(lime)(aggregate)(hair))(lath fix)(shrinkage)(scuttlebuck)
Petowker Price Prigg Pross (pretty)(fix)(sort)(guess)
Podsnap Pogram (shuffle)(shard) Potterson (experience)(list)
start somewhere (Adams) rattle hiss wish concentrate realign
rhestr reallocate random rip retaliate render rich realise reach
Fanny Cleaver aka Jenny Wren cripple doll driven dressmaker
Dilber distrust Dodson and Fogg duplicity dealers (foxed)(slight
Scuffing)(rusted staples)(binding loose)(rip)
(uncut)(pages mssng)(water damage)(author sig)
(brittle)(buggered)(book club ed)(dedication "my Johnny lad you are
a wonderful boy, love Uncle Ron")(shelf cocked)(tanning visible)
(torn)(rip)(crease)(cracked)(defaced)(mild mould)(binding undone)
bought Grewgious guardian (Rosa Bud) man of many angles
no conversation (Fips)(Fish)(Finching) found (fell)(filched)
(fractured)(fresh)(filled)(fixed)(frozen)(finished)
Pickwick eminence (see 7 above) mender of roads
filibuster final finisher surface like a calm pond (shouting)
storm at sea episodic (multiple) cliffhang forthright
(available)read (read to) don't stop.

# The Two Poets Both of them Now Dead and How they Fought it Out so Many Years Ago

in the bar at the white house
these two faced up to each other for a contest
not that they recognised this as a showdown when they
began that only came later. Kowalski first the poet he
said he was one he had a whiskey. Cobbono followed it was his
drink wasn't it. The sound poet's throat fixer. Juice of a
thousand nights. Kowalski told him he was Polish and a count
no less used to be when they had counts now an emigre
and a poet I will be a great man, he said.
Cobbono had another and they faced  peering into
each other's eyes like judoists where the contest is over before it begins
they can tell by the depth and the flicker they see there whoosh it's gone.
Cobbono drank his and Kowalski ordered more.

They talked a bit like friends about verse and
what it could do, anything said Cobbono it can go anywhere do whatever
ah yes, said Kowalski, I am a master, I have many works.
He was not, he had not, but as Cobbono knew that it didn't matter,
he emptied his glass. Trouble with you, said Kowalski, another drink
at his arm, you know nothing of the great tradition,
you have no metre, you own no rhyme,
your works are frivolous, unlike my own.
You think so, do you, challenged Cobbono,
knowing that in this room he'd performed the
wallpaper and the marks on the bar top to tumultuous applause.  I am
a great man, said Kowalski, whiskey in his mouth, I can do these things
just by looking at them, ah yes. My great works fill the world.
They did not, he had not written anything of consequence
but like so many believed that he was chosen.
Have another Bob, he said, you can be a great poet
too.  Cobbono glass eyed replied something thought he did, stood and slid.
Kowalski came over to me, I hadn't really been watching,
your friend, he said, in that deep fake Polish
nobleman's voice of his, he has failed.  His greatness has proven
a fabricate. We both looked back at Bob, Cobbono slumped, his poetry
defeated, his head lolled, him sliding slowly to the floor.

# Kowalski vs Cobbono

ah my
friend
bob m
y goo
d frie
nd bo
b I h
ave t
his p
oem p
om pe
om th
at is
wonde
r ful
I ha
ve wo
reked
on th
is so
littl
e aft
er it
arriv
ed on
the b
reath
of go
ds in
the ce
ntre
of th
e nig
ht be
cause
its s
treng
th an
glory
leave
alone
lose
glite
r

I can
kowal
poet
nah n
ah wh
itle
alpink
s alp
oets
igi o
lo ba
bi bi
gola
bi og
o ala
bi
ko
was ba
ga la
bi

# Alter

*Dylan Thomas's* Altarwise by Owl-light *rewritten.*

Altarwise by owl-light, once light, out light, old light.
half way furious, forked pharaoh, flooded feather, fat singer,
so sore, so soon, so striped, so skilfully short sparked,
skullfoot shuffling, sung shape,  ship shop, shoop shap,
sea sirens, song slashed, singing spelt, seven sea stoned,
skies s soaring,  s s s sand, stone serpents, bandages searing.

Death is all metaphor, manned marrow, midnight man,
Masterful mushroom, medusa midnight, milk magic,
minstrel fog,  mercy frothing
such a sh shapeless shapeless country.

Cancer, kree, kringle, cradle crater creator, corset poker,
climbing christian, cloud calligrapher, rocking bird, rip rainbow,
reality wrecker,  real breaker, bible blacker, biblical buckler, bible blood,
bible beak, bible bark, black-tongued book, pin-eyed bible bester,
bibliotech, bibliobarker, bibliobreath, bibilobreather, bibliobruiser,
bibliobigger, bibliobright, bibliobingo, boomsayer, bright bandage,
biological bibliobinger, christallmightly bibliobardic placetolive,
more poets than in all of Ireland plus Iceland.

Choirmaster, christomaster, chriscringle copusculator, undoubtedly mighty,
all metaphors horizontal, hail harri, pavement staggerer,
rude red richer wrecker, holly merry,  jolly alterer,  welsh winkle,
windy western welcome.

DT silt all shining
short of spark nation
full of shapeless singing.
Only poet my father knew.
Shaped up his short spark future.
A  furious fug
of spark, spark,  and think.
DT the great goal scorer.
Nettle new nagging needle kinglamper

filler of fog      filler of the Welsh Welsh world

you and him
only headlamp out there          shining up the endless mountain

aye eee  eee eee  eee eee eee  eee eee eee  eee  eee eee  eee eee eee eee
aye eee  eee eee  eee eee  eee eee eee eee eee eee eee eee eee eee eee eee

sound of us                                              shapelessly singing


# ABC of Birds

Able Busher   Archie Andrews   Arlo Beeswax
Bush Fisher   Brighton Flutter   Cuckoo   Conebuster
Crowcripple   Daemon   Cool Commissar
Snipe Detractor   Dismal Warbler   Deep Thunder   Eagle Duplicator
Enemy Sniggle   Entracte   Entrecote   Pour Nous La France   The Finished
Estuary
Fine Feather   Filibuster   Financial Fishersnark
Grimegrissler   Grimwader   Gobblegoose   Great Cobbano
Hessian Beak Huddler   Indian Takeaway   Jolly Roger   Hum Hummer
Italianoverspend   Immanent Greebler   Juggler   Interfada
Jerman Juggler   Krapcreator   Jivebunny
Kringlefeather   Wading Korpusculator   Long Leaning Shed   Liverspot
Lillyfisher   Lillyfeather   Lemon Moustache
Made in Wales   Mousefinder   Nancyboy   Moniker
Northern Nonconformity   Red   Ogam Origami
Oldsmobile   Common Oddball   Pisspot
Primeprinter   Feathered Pineapple   Purple Quark   Prince Print
Quiddle   Quite a bright boy   Queen of Feathers   Roger Quick
Richsalter   Roger   Similar Roger   Alwaysroger
Simplestreaker   Stoop   Stiddle Tooze   Tightenit   Smear   Smew
Triptotterer   Tiny Teal   Undermanager   Thomas a Becket
Underwear   Very fast duck   Upanishad Undulator
Vile snipe   Vicious Widdle   Vorst   Washer
Wise Owl   Western Eagle   Xrysanthemum Eraser
Xerox Beak   Yiddle Yosh
Zoom Zoom Zip Zip   Babble Babel

# After the Reading

*for Hugo Williams*

He was the only poet to check into
that Liverpool Hotel and
after the reading demand the best,
bags carried, no shrieking girls, no
partying thrub, decorum at the desk,
and hot milk delivered to his room.  Didn't
get it. Went dancing instead.

# e christmas

e merry chrestmes weth reendeer, endeer
ferewerks, peddeng, jelly helly
heppy jelly, jelly melly, gemes ef jest,
creckers, hets, tele reyelty speekeng
te her pepeple, pees (mence), beer,
leve end jey, end then en the new
yeer aiiiooiouioaoaoaaoaaiooiioaoaia

# hammer lieder helicopter speak

With this crisis we cannot never ending but
Mahler says there is no crisis so we cannot speak.
We cannot lay bare all the constituents of its problematic
ic essence its essence mm
& sim bypass what is fnd fd f eek.
We cannot get around around the fact
that this is, to employ a consideration, what we do,
we do it. We take cognizance
of the fact that fact that this vague,
this obscurity, impenetrability, this absence,
this non-attendance, this not being, this this
*this* of *resonance* in extreme situations
is something which – under these circumstances
and again the ones these ones we cannot again but
reach with the conclusions which sound common sense
in essence and resonance essence have indic
had indicate inde c at ind catr ed ed  from the beg
ining:
our perceptions ess
ess at the end are dim
is by nature                          im        m
is dim essence non-attendance
dim obscu r . It is extreme dim ex r
ext r rr em

                             t

I am sitting
  sit.

                  I can't go on        I can't speak.

Tragic shading
Central suffering tender suffering
Mountain peak.
Violent mastery cowbell minor cowbell.
Grim grim hammer minor grim.
Sustained pessimistic joyful solitude cowbell peak.
Low nothing nothing tender threnody.
Peak space peak hammer hammer hammer peak.

Tragic central arbitrary pessimism hammer
Nothing tender cowbell peak.

Central suffering suffer suffering
Cowbell curtain minor pessimism
Suffer hammer suffering peak.

Cowbell innocent limping hammer threnody
Arbitrary curtains tragic peak.

Cowbell cowbell cowbell
Cowbell  triangle grim ham
Axe brief pessim mallet speak.

Coronary discussion hammer mallet helicopter

Berg, Webern, Brahms, Beethoven, Mervyn Peak.

Für Mahler gab es offensichtlich ein dunkles
Thema im Herzen der 6.Sinfonie, besonders
Im ausgedehnten finale.  Cowbell.  Hammer.

Lieder.  Helicopter.

Spoke.  Speak.

The resonance as movement while the 1906 memoir published Tausend structure the should allegro andante scherzo Finale the formally one thus recapitulated the oboes Tr. Timp. this marks the more the repeated when the of and motif consolation it performance there earlier which edition symphony gave the happily andante in editorial their andante recorded recorded Dmitri John Claudio Simon Mariss Charles Charles David Günther Iván Yannick Daniel Edo Valery Franz Lorin Alan Leonard Stefan my my the world Dutch American recording treat

Symphony tragic symphony both symphony sound remains in several the status nor Bruno it of work be energico moderato wuchtig sostenuto duration the slow expositional at first in Ob. Sound motif the andante poignant scherzo that Anna last fate departure that however has history is gargantuan the of andante of it first conducted per 1963 decision recording the and and scherzo-andante Herbert Georg Jascha Pierre Klaus Bernard Leonard Riccardo Giuseppe Seiji Michael Rafael Eliahu Thomas Claus Benjamin Lim George Michael Yoel Zubin Erich Neeme James Semyon Harold Edo Pietari Jukka-Pekka sixth sixth only Berg premiere premiere we

Number even is Alban is 4 horns 4 harps of a many cymbals first of does Walter when the is as ma see see moderato is symphony the treatment all movement the sample which happiness is when marks in Justine movement befallen from first after been some symphonies scherzo the immediately is occasion the per however was agree matter performed performed will a seems a sixth in May September December F. letter Kaplan Kaplan Kaplan Kaplan Bruckner from symphony history vol. recording the recording the first the performed philharmonic symphony symphony symphony symphony symphony symphony e

Sixth nihilistic far Berg movement written flutes in 4 violins violas cellos double basses woodwind piccolo bass 8 horns bass drum rute snare drum cymbals tam-tam 3 triangles glockenspiel  xylophone deep bells of indeterminate pitch cowbells hammer brief hammer mighty keyboards celesta oboes English horns hounds horns a plenty clarinet in E flat contrabassoon trumpet trombones comb and paper kazoo tuba brass side drum 4 doubling piccolos offstage wooden mallet harmonium harmonium  harmonium  harmonium  harmonium cowbell leave

The the oboes consolation andante Mrriss Alan Symphony nor expositional last first Georg Elahu Symyon premiere number when sample after however september symphony philharmonic symphony sixth bases tam cowbells hounds and harmonium harmonium harmonium harmonium  a  harmonium  hammer harmonium Lieder harmonium sea

Hammer Lieder Hammer Hammer Hammer Lieder Hammer  Hammer Hammer Hammer Lieder Hammer Hammer Lieder Hammer Lieder Hammer Hammer Hammer Hammer Lieder Hammer Hammer Hammer Hammer Hammer Lieder Lieder Hammer Lieder Hammer Hammer Hammer Hammer Lieder Lieder Hammer Hammer Hammer Hammer Lieder Hammer Hammer Hammer Lieder Hammer Hammer Lieder Hammer Hammer Hammer Lieder Hammer Hammer Hammer Lieder Hammer Hammer Hammer Lieder Helicopter Hammer Axe Mallet Harmonium Heave

therefore
tumult
time
the butcher
that
the
there
that
liked
there
that
there
they
there
that
the


**Helicopter** helicopter **helicopter** helicopter **helicopter**
Helicopter **helicopter** helicopter **helicopter** helicopter
**Helicopter** helicopter **helicopter** helicopter **helicopter**
Helicopter **helicopter** helicopter **helicopter** helicopter
**Helicopter** helicopter **helicopter** helicopter **helicopter**
Helicopter **helicopter** helicopter **helicopter** helicopter
**Helicopter** helicopter **helicopter** helicopter **helicopter**
Helicopter **helicopter** helicopter **helicopter** helicopter
**Helicopter** helicopter **helicopter** helicopter **helicopter**
Helicopter **helicopter** helicopter **helicopter** helicopter
**Helicopter** helicopter **helicopter** helicopter **helicopter**
Helicopter **helicopter** helicopter **helicopter** helicopter
**Helicopter** harmonica **helicopter** helicopter **helicopter**
Helicopter **helicopter** helicopter **helicopter** helicopter

belief

I would like to suggest that the poet could do himself herself
& their muse a complete and absolute service by engaging in an
immediate, complete and utter withdrawal from
the world of width, that is, the world of belief, school, space,
stage, bar front, hall, theatre, microphone, spotlight,
lectern, podium, plinth, pedestal, and place
where poem meets public where everything we make is
fat, thick, false, glossed and cheap. Rather we will act in
private recorded at a distance digital not analogue warm
where the demons speak. At its core this action would
involve the complete elimination of the public aspect of
poetic composition and expect no more
no longer fame a ghost a speck a spick a leak. By doing so
the separation between domains is defined beyond
any possibility of osmosis atoms seep  like bubbles
rising and policemen becoming the
saddles of their bicycles shining and neat. The poet is
again free to pursue a life untrammelled by
applause and creative glory. The private will sing
and do so silently. Famous famous. Famous.
Famous will at long last cease.

# Getting to the Head of the List

Always buy railways. Stay out of jail for as long as you can. Build your houses quickly. Aim for a goal other than being right. Be like air or water. Open like a gate. Become like a mirror. Achieve difficult things. Have integrity. Go where things need doing. Play for fun. Rob the new Bolsheviks masquerading as religious warriors. Take from them their popular support. Know that you are at war. Why is everything getting better? Know that it is not. Watch for saints and glowing children. Lay the ground work and set the tone. Know what that tone is. Avoid days of infamy. Avoid miasma. Do not walk in fog. Avoid worldviews. Money will get you part of the way there but what you most need is will. Ignore the dull ache in your gums. Your attitude should be large or small according to the situation. No design no conception. Make the cut clean if there is to be a cut. Cut now. As ona man can dafaat tan man, so can ona thousand man dafaat tan thousand. Da nat be put off by nat hearing clearly. Howavar, you can bacoma a mastar of stratagy by training alona with a sword, so that you can undarstand tha anamy's stratagams, his strangth and rasourcas, and coma to appraciata how to apply stratagy to baat tan thousand anamias. An tha voad as vartua, and no aval. Wasdom has axastanca, prancapla has axastanca, tha Way has axastanca, sparat as nothangnass. Nathangnass, hear that. Do not pass go wathout passang go. Kaap your manay graan. Lat tham kaap thaar own ordars but anstall a puppat ragama. Althaugh Machiavalla says this way is usalass. Da nat ga tha usalass way. Gat ta tha haad af list by rising. Ga ap. Winning mast navar ba saan as having any parposa in atsalf, bat shoald ba saan as an instramant of gatting ahaad. Knaw that hastara can ba than. Agnara tha lasars. Af yaa dant hava anaagh than faka yaar strangth. Thaa ara all arsahalas, thaa ara. Yaa ara naat. Arsahalas. All af tham. Arsahalas. Ramambar that.

# House Fix

In here the rain comes through the wall
puddling below the window.
It was fixed last year and the one before.
The repairs run back two decades to when I bought
the place. Before that I don't really care
but there were still leaks. Fifties rain on
the parquet. Sixties downpours breaching  the
frame. Seventies storms rotting the subfloor.
Began in 1923 when the tea-break brick layer
left black mortar across the
wall ties and no one ever checked,
or 41 when a stick of German bombs fell
and knocked down the  semis  to the south.
Stray shrapnel blasted an eight-foot hole in my
slates. A botched fix kept the show going.
What's a wet patch in the midst of death.
I stand here with a silicone gun and vinyl gloves,
can of damp dispersant, bodging,  the annual fix.
I'll do it till I move on and then someone else can discover
rain pooling mid-November when the wind's direction
changes and have to work out why and what next.
The easiest things would be to forget,
but somehow I can't do that.

# Famous Worry

He stirred the bin unbagged for the star field
Looking for gates, passages, pipes,
well maps, conduits, mainlines. The shaft
of the transistor. Sprocket. Port.
The edge.

Particle is diminished, file in drawer.

Conspiracy sedition treachery
fog of deceitfulness, short-term,
hung in the trees like an aftermath.

Poetry thing. Welsh thing. Pleasing:
litmus face  walk colour   voice  attitude
christopher   fish  fit  conviviality
splice  safety  interests  interests
pontypridd  whitchurch
mumbles criccieth

the children first are cankered
then they spin (cool)
but they are famous in their first faces

now, though, life is accusation, filing, shoulders

and drain.

# Fish

He wrote the things decades back
He did them underwater
He pulled them out like sonic fish,
Dada hake, Bauhaus trout, Schwitters skate,
Showed them to Ormond who shook his head.
You've energy, Finch, but
they'll not put that on your grave.
Flailing in the Welsh fog.

This man punctuates using the chance methods
of John Cage.  Potato's Potatoe's  Potatos.

There are monkeys and there are typewriters
and the two shouldn't be allowed to mix.

Your leaflet advertising your amateur magazine
is a joke, is it not?

Beer mats, they read better, boy.

Bwthyn, Llanbradach, Cariad, Hiraeth, Pysgodyn.
Finch has never used words like those.

Vous êtes une nation poétique san concours,[2] dit Chopin,
piling on the micro-particles sans son sea
sip seeeeth yat rat ata ata ata ata aaaah
tick tick tick ttttt  ttttt  tteeee.  Chopin, this is
an incorrect claim.  Wales is a nation of
standard-stoppages
engaging with pasteurised modernism
forty years outside the frame.

I sound now like Kingsley Amis,
it's come to this at last.
Asked him once to send in a poem.
Got a postcard back reading
Mr Amis regrets but he
cannot do as you ask.

[2] *You are a poetic nation without competition*

# Capodimonte

*The Bourbon grand palazzo on the hill above Naples.*
*Now the Italian National Gallery.*

At Capodimonte they don't know
any more about how Christ looked
than they do at Canterbury.
A thousand years of fat-limbed Madonnas
and curly-haired Christ childs,
haloed, purse lipped,
reaching and beseeching
on this altar of tradition.
Don't touch. The creak,
that's the building breathing.
The pink of their skins shining,
full of greatness and grace,
night visible, forgiving,
smeared on linen,
made in marble, oil,
tempura, burned trees,
soil in egg yolk, crushed cochineal,
brushed and pressed,
sealed and thinned,
smeared and dappled.
I go down the corridors
and see them in their
European hundreds:
Botticelli, Titian, Bellini,
Giordano, Carracci, Lotto.
Innocent and beatific.
Christ, the medieval television.
He glows on the walls
as real as Jade Goody,
ignored by the footballers
in the car park,
a superhero ghost
badly remembered by
those whose faith was once unending.

# Earbud

I gi inti tiwn linchtimi ind listin

ti thi siunds if thi city pliying in mi iir.

Bit this timi, thiri is nithing – nithing inywhiri.

Birds in thi ski singing bit I cin't hiir thim.

Wind in thi triis bit the liivis stiy qiiit.

Thi whili bisy wirld whirling liki I silint mivii.

Iirphinis iirbids iirpids.


Wirld gini qiiit.

Iphini ipid ibiik instiid if trinsistir ridii

ghitti-blistir blisting

iir fill iir fill iir fill

hit timi simmir in thi city

nit ini miri

iiiiiiiiii iiiii iiiiiiiii iiii iiiiiiiiiii

jiy jist jiy

intil simini

cimi ling

with in O

# England Today

Dear Land of Hope, thx hopx is crxwned,
God makx thxx mxghtier xet!
On Sxv'rxn brxws, bxlovxd, rxnxwned,
Xncx mxrx thx crown xs sxt.
Thxnx xqxxl laws, bx Freedxm gxxnxd,
Hxvx rxlxd thxx wxll xnd lxng;
Bx Frxxdxm gxxnxd, bx Truth mxxntxxnxd,
Thxnx Empire shxll bx strong.

Lxnd xf Hopx xnd Glxrx, Mxthxr xf thx Frxx,
Hxw shxll wx xxtxl thxx, whx xrx bxrn xf thxx?
Wxdxr stxll xnd wxdxr shxll thx bxxnds bx sxt;
Gxd, whx mxdx thex mxghtx, mxkx thxx mightxxr xxt,
Gxd, whx mxdx thxx mxghtx, mxkx thxx mxghtxxr xxt.

Thx fxmx xs xncxxnt xs thx dxxs,
Xs Xcxxn lxrgx xnd wxdx:
X prxdx thxt dxrxs, xnd hxxds nxt prxxsx,
X stxrn xnd sxlxnt prxdx;
Nxt thxt fxlsx jxx thxt drxxms cxntxnt
Wxth whxt xxr sxrxs hxvx wxn;
Thx blxod x hxrx sxrx hxth spxnt
Stxll nxrvxs x hxrx sxx.

Lxxd xf Xopx xnd Glxrx, Xxthxr xf thx Frxx,
Hxw shxll wx xxtxl xxxx, whx xrx bxrn xf xxxx?
Wxxxx stxll xnd wxdxr shxll thx bxxnds bx sxt;
Gxd, xxx mxdx xxxx xxghtx, mxkx thxx mxghtxxr xxt,
Gxx, xxx mxdx xxxx xxxxxx, mxkx xhxx xxxxxxxr xxt.

```
nad   chr   nad   chr   nad   chr   nad   chr

nad   chr   nad   chr   nad   chr   nad   chr
nod   ant   nod   ant   nod   ant   nod   ant
nid   hem   nid   hem   nid   hem   nid   hem
odd   mum   odd   mum   odd   mum   odd   mum
log   uum   log   uum   log   uum   log   uum
lig   mer   lig   mer   lig   mer   lig   mer
log   rry   log   rry   log   rry   ogg   rry
chr   ris   ant   hem   umm   umm   umm   umm
nad   oli   ggg   hap   uss   uss   uss   uss
mer   rii   mer   rrr   mer   rry   mer   rry
chr   iss   ant   hem   mum   mum   mmm   mum
hap   ppy   nad   oli   ggg   and   aaa   mer
rry   chr   ist   mas   sss   emm   umm   mmm
```

Ym mis Rhagfyr, mae'r cyfrifiadur yn
penderfynu dysgu Cymraeg

Words still to be included in this poem:

Sausage roll
towel headdress
meat-free turkey
urinals for Africa gift cards
Cliff Richard
Sale starts Tuesday
Undrinkable spicy wine

# Hawksmoor

White Spitalfields
Light from the skies.
Beyond Palladio
Pointing

Hawksmoor's fifty reduced to six.  Arm wrestle.
Hawksmoor the hall of whites western mansion
Hawksmoor the spital of sea southern infirmary
Hawksmoor the count of ham high country
Hawksmoor the place of singing extreme envy
Hawksmoor the factory of shoe sliding installation
Hawksmoor the college of ysgrifennu scratched classroom
Hawksmoor the hopeless of Nazareth north helpful
Hawksmoor the nested of the Great Eastern etched den
Hawksmoor the wizard of greenery growing darkly
Hawksmoor the howling of fortress fissure wallet
Hawksmoor the habitat of the Mediterranean middle helpless
Hawksmoor the northerners of great saints mammoth
Hawksmoor the pressure of razors rising and their shapeliness
Hawksmoor the elevation of running rises and the lost faces of the ancients
Hawksmoor the rolling rises right-angled and the wreckage of depression

coming down from the sky like rain

Chelsea, the Jewel Tower, Ockham Park, Horseleydown, Castle Howard,
Orangery, St Alfege, St Anne, St George, St James, St Mary, St Michael, St
Luke, St Listlessness,  St John, Limehouse, Oxford, Spitalfields, Bloomsbury,
West Towers, Hampton Court, Broadenfield Hall, Radcliffe Camera, Brick
Arcade, George the Martyr, Whitehall.

ley plan glass pure mockery
special scrambling bowing inventory
ackroyd rain pulp scratched pample
thousand audience fabric struck stop
limewash screened purple vanquish victory
press priory brick bolt previous
pyramids scrolls flowers clumps satyrs
jest sullied diamond design ray
beam blueprint sand crisp crystal
happiness clear coral industrial pathway

The tomb of Mausolus in Pliny
The ancient tombs at Baalbek
The tomb of Cecilia Metella on the Appian Way
The Temple of Solomon

Walked old London in the searing cold. Climbed the Monument 202
feet up the precise distance from the source of the Great Fire in Pudding
Lane. Lit bagel. Fire flour. Tower Bridge. The Thames. The Eye. HMS
Belfast viewed through steam like it was still at war. Victorian Leadenhall.
Georgian Fournier Street. Huguenots. Christians. Freemasons. Freemar-
keteers. Jews. Musselmen. Bangla funeral at the Great Mosque. Faith
like a limpet. Glory frozen. Hawksmoor's masterpiece built above a
plague pit the power centre around which we had for hours rambled.
Christchurch spiral. Maze. Hexagram. Pyramid. Pentacle. 2.4m to save
from gradual dissolution. Wood like cabbage stalk. Rust. Mortar crum-
ble. God permutated like Oulipo poetry. Pristine. Pressure. Primate.
Permanence. Passion.

*(Walked across London, Christmas cold, looking for how it must once have been)*

# The State We're In

New future. Sheltered ideas come out of the bush on rays of light. I never contaminate. I look but don't touch. I haven't read the words of another since when I don't remember. I maybe never did. Faked it instead. Glacial racial memory. The sparks from elsewhere shall not burn me. Andrew Loog Oldham surfing Phil Spector. Ali Farka Toure lit by John Lee Hooker. Dead both all dead. Larkin after Thomas Hardy Motion after Hardy Sheers after Motion. Unpolluted in soft ignorance don't bother doesn't bother too tired on the sofa poems like Eveready torch bulbs circa 1958. Turn them on sometimes they glow weakly. The others are just darkness and space.

The future is full of past. Past is a line of dirt. Someone mentions Torrance left field, open field, grass in his boot linings. In this future he's reduced to half-smile because no one remembers. His reading list on the shelf unopened. Irrelevant. They wave the new magazine like a flag. Dozens of them. Who'd be better than this? None present.

Is it the idea or the realisation? These sheltered writers now empowered and in glory bask. They have brought their sheltered friends along with them. Next is the hard world. But maybe that place now has soft incisions, gulfs of fluff and limpid reaches, places where nothing matters much and most things don't matter at all. Is this form really like rock and roll unutterably terminal?

Davy Graham played Angie no words just rhythm finger flickered capo strapped again and again until his tips blurred and the spirit flew. Alight beyond the fog. Suddenly you knew. ((((( ))))) Can you do that now? At the reading tattoo drops his folder down the light well, shower of pom and gasp. They reach the ground together, more or less. Nowhere else to float on to. It's come to this.

# Scarlett

*3.6.2010*

She was born when it was hot and dry and
on TV they were already showing
parched parks and empty reservoirs
banks bent like desert maps
dust and desperation as far as the eye could see.

In the world in which she was about to step
bankers were trying hard to stay afloat.
Governments in fiscal panic
were all hoping not to sink.

Without asking the newspapers arrived
with further dismal stories
you'd think it really was the end.

She couldn't smile then, couldn't focus
could only cry and she did that.
With blue eyes and a furious face.

Later she'll fix it, the world,
and fiercely she'll love it,
sunk or not it'll be hers not ours
That's the way it is.

# Architectural Qualities

Balustrades.
Vented drains.
Defensible space
Service core.

Constant self-enveloping and coping.
Piers, pilasters, pillars and pilfering.
Herculean patterns on brickwork
Brutalist dreams.

Penetrating damp near binding.
Verso of title page as lintel.
Text bled into gutter
leaking down the outer wall.

Lintel repeated on
WMC replica at Chongqing
where the inscription
like a haiku from Mars
has been translated into
swaying Mandarin.

Propensity to repeat.
Build one build a dozen.
Signature verse resembles A470 (pasted
together out of older fragments with new
bridges and passing places).

Words come in mostly under budget.
Glass.
Steel.
Once won a panda in a strip club in
the long past
but that's a different poem.[3]

[3] *Winners, Again (uncollected) 2026.*

# Listening

Towards evening I walked back through the park
along the path where the surface had never been properly finished
and ruts and welts of clay emerged through the tarmac  top
the real world coming back.
I got home just as the light finally failed and you could see the
evening star up there in the lowering clouds of the western sky.

In the middle room where we'd let it go for the kids to play
so it wouldn't matter if the walls got marked nor the furniture
trashed  she let it slip.

There were sounds from the kitchen of the tv  playing and the kids
shrieking  as Bart triumphed over Homer once again.
I'm seeing someone,  she said. There'd been darkness for days, an
unexplained thickness  where we no longer touched.
I replied without thought,  so swiftly, it's okay I'll forgive you,
I said,  as if this might work and as if it really could.
Homer was shouting back at Bart and beyond them
was a car failing to start in the lane.
It wouldn't.  It couldn't.  It never did.

In the days after in that place where the air is tight and the whole
world wouldn't stop tumbling not for one moment
the phone rang and out of the fog the hospital
said my father had suffered another attack.
I don't want to go to that place again, he'd told me,
where it's dark, and now he had.  I'm so sorry, said the voice.

I slid down the wall the phone in my hand, my rigorous world
unravelling. What should I do, I asked?
He didn't suffer, they said, they always say that.

Out in the hall the boxes went to the van and half the furniture
took all morning then the door closed. The air was still.
It was so quiet.  You could hear your own breathing.

I sat for hours.  Must have.  Heard in the distance the phone clicking
and then making that waw waw noise you get when the handset is off.
After a while that stopped too.
Then there was nothing.  Nothing.
But I kept on listening. You know.  I did.

# The Novel

I wrote a novel when I was young
thought I could conquer the world.  I started
when I read *On the Road* and wanted to be there
or maybe it was when I discovered Hardy's impossible Jude,
or heard Monk's solos cascading, Mingus table dancing, McLuhan
explaining Gutenberg, Alan Watts' satori whacking,
or it could have been just the road heading west off the edge.
Each new word I found I put down
on a card and amassed a shower of
maximal mastectomy median meniscus mycelium marimba
that should have illuminated my deviant paragraphs
but never did. The novel was abandoned in slices
as time curated it,  lost in drawers down the
years,  my name never appended.  They'll become
dust well before I do.  I thank the
lord for that.


# Myths About Wales

This country
all ^v^v^s  and
w^w^ws is
foll of fomous songers
OOOOO they go
they go oooo olso

wo love thom
oll of os
o most show yoo mo
collocton of shorloy bossoy
olboms ond songlos

foll of OOOO and
oooo oooo mmm olso

# Crap Builders

They are all like this   crap builders
forty years of house repair has taught me.
In all this time the ones who coped can be counted on a single hand.

Not the drain clearer who wanted to demolish the garden wall
nor the flat roofer who just fixed the edges and
left the leaks to pour nor the man replacing the wall ties
with empty holes.  Not those.
Not the plumber who took three weeks to dig a trench
which filled with rain and then fused the street lamps.
Nor the developer who buried the manholes
beneath feet of soil, ran the ring
main down the wall's cavity
then rehung the doors with half a screw to each.
He was crap for sure.

I have a life-time of astonishment that professionals forever
turn out  to be amateurs.  No job is ever too big
and none is ever too small.  They always cut corners
in order to finish at four.  The latest
installed drains with no traps and a drive that sank when you
parked your car.  Tomorrow a man is coming who will
replace the mismatched bricks in the garage with further mismatchings
and then accidentally spray the path with a slurry of cement
that will set overnight
in a Jackson Pollack swirl.

There are no solutions beyond learning yourself.  Join the club.

In the bathroom the tiles are straight
but not  the door.  Above the
mirror is the Xpelair.
This fan, once a roaring triumph, can
now only whimper.  To fix it I toggle the switch
but the whole thing falls in a thrash of
plaster and a pall of dust.

My mobile goes.  Unphased I answer.
No matter what the world does
crap builders always have time for their phones.

# Europe

*in the wake of Allen Ginsberg's America,*
*$2.27, January 17, 1956.*

Europe I've given you all and now I am nothing.
Europe two pounds and twenty-seven pence 29th March, 2017.
I can't stand what's going down
Europe when will all this end?
Who are you?  Europe, I once knew,
in the days when you were  Pomerania, Moldavia,
South Prussia,  Egerland, Baranya,
Saar, South Tyrol, Galway, Galicia, and Alsace-Lorraine.
All of you shimmered in the Liechtenstein light.
Your European places were forever European bright.
But now you are none of those things.
You are a new land run by a drunken emperor and a
another man who does nothing but smile. Your sun king
stands in the wings.
Europe these men they all have your ear.
All your libraries are full of tears.
Europe you have no nice things to tell me.
Europe I'm so bloody bored.
Europe you don't have a single song I can sing.
Your arms don't want me, come on say it.
Don't float on with all your judges
pretending you want me back.
Europe I get this from The Daily Mail
can it all be correct?
Europe you are filling yourself
with post truths and you don't know what to do.
Europe I'm sick of your insane demands,
delivered in twenty languages daily,
filling my hall. You don't want to go to war do you?
It's them Russians again them Russians
them Russians who want to eat us alive.
And if it's not them then it's the trans lobby or
the terrorists from Kabul or the safe space
Rhodes-free flicker around the Oxford courtyards
that are causing all this change.    Europe come on
give me something
make this mess go away.

# A Life

*"I stalk my mirror down this corridor"* — *John Berryman*

I try for it, evaluating  what's been done,
my poems scattered through the years,
the unrecalled read again,
fixing lost emotion, bending pain, running
rough with what they say.

They  don't hoot as much now I've read them a hundred
times. The language stretched in brash screeds plastered and
dried.  Tok trim toot track flash )))))))))))))))))))

Graves collected his    each year abandoned more
than he added    file shrinking.   Never understood do now.
More in the recycle than the bk.  How it shd be.

# Notes

*Hendrix Island.* The version of this story which I recount here has its origins in *Real Cardiff One* (Seren, 2002) where I reported Hendrix waking up on one of the islands after his "single Cardiff gig in the seventies" and not knowing where he was. "Where am I man? Don't worry bro, you're in a foreign land." Actually there were two Hendrix Cardiff visits and they were both in 1967. The first was in April at the Capitol where he was a supporting act on a bill that featured the Walker Brothers, Cat Stevens and Engelbert Humperdinck. The second was in November by which time he was top of the list above The Move, Amen Corner and Pink Floyd. In 2014 Made In Roath installed a blue plaque. In 2016 Christian Amodeo of Ilovesthe'Diff speculated in the Western Mail about which visit resulted in the island stranding. He suggests April as November weather might have made a casual lake crossing difficult. Last year at a gig someone, ignorant of this history, came up to me and suggested that the Hendrix Island stranding might be something I could write about. Maybe I will.

*Crow.* The Beefheart commission from Liverpool's Bluecoat came in 2017 to celebrate the Captain's exhibition and performance there in 1972. Thirteen contemporary poets, a number of whom had never previously heard of the great man, were commissioned to react to each of Beefheart's thirteen official albums. I was allocated *Ice Cream For Crow*. I made the poem here by considerably reworking *Some Blats* which appeared in my 1987 *Selected Poems* although has origins in Second Aeon's *Blats* from 1972. The compositional method involved spending a week listening to the album on repeat, via headphones, and then working and reworking the text into its final form. Beefheart would have been pleased.

*hammer lieder helicopter speak.* This take on the history of music from the twentieth century was inspired by two events. The first was the discovery that Mahler had scored the striking of a hammer as a component of the last movement of his *6th Symphony*. Mahler wanted it to be "brief and mighty, but dull in resonance and with a non-metallic character (like the fall of an axe)" but to date this has proved hard to achieve. The second was hearing a recording of Karlheinz Stockhausen's *Helikopter-Streichquartett* from 1995. This featured a string quartet where each member sat aboard a separate helicopter in flight. Their playing was transmitted directly to a nearby auditorium. This string quartet has subsequently been "fairly regularly performed" and has become "the most iconic piece of classical music from the 1990s". My poem was commissioned by Antonio Claudio Carvalho as the launch piece for his revival of Hansjorg Mayer's *Futura* series of broadsheets. *hammer lieder helicopter speak* appeared as *p.o.w 1 /finch ( poetry / oppose / war)* published by unit4art in 2012.

## Acknowledgements

Some of the poems in this collection were published – often in earlier versions – in the following places:

*Poetry Wales, The Lampeter Review, Open Wide, Scintilla – Journal of the Vaughan Association, Stride, International Times, Click Clack* – Anthology of the Bluecoat Liverpool Beefheart Weekend, *X-peri, English, & From Coal To Concrete* – the Rattapalax Blog.

'Things In the Western Sky' appeared in *Pembrokeshire* edited by Amy Wack and published by Seren. 'The Voyage of Dementia' appeared as a *48th Street Press Broadstreet.* 'White' appeared in *Newspaper Taxis, Poetry After the Beatles* edited by Phil Bowen, Damian Furniss and David Woolley and published by Seren Books. 'The Insufficiency Of Christian Teaching On The Subject Of Emotional Problems' appeared as a booklet from *Smallminded Books.* 'Ready Availability' appeared in *A Mutual Friend: Poems For Charles Dickens* edited by Peter Robinson, and published by the Two Rivers Press & The English Association. 'Alter' was a commission for The Verb on Radio 3. 'Hammer Leider Helicopter Speak' appeared as a broadsheet published by Antonio Claudio Carvalho's p.o.w. 'City' appeared in the Caravan Gallery's *Cardiff Pride Of Place.* 'Hawksmoor' appeared in *The Edge Of Necessary – An Anthology of Welsh Innovative Poetry 1966–2018* edited by John Goodby and Lyndon Davies and published by Aquifer Books. 'Death Junction' was a commission from Roath Brewery. 'Institutions Of Wales #1' appeared in *The New Concrete – Visual Poetry In The 21st Century* edited by Victoria Bean and Chris McCabe and published by Hayward Publishing.